VIOLINJUDY'S

THE ACCIDENTAL AXOLOTL

INTRODUCING SHARPS, FLATS & NATURALS

SUPPLEMENTARY SONGS

FOR BEGINNING-INTERMEDIATE VIOLIN LEARNERS

Violin Judy's

VERY FUN VIOLIN COLLECTION

The Accidental Axolotl by Judy Naillon

Copyright © 2024 ViolinJudy

www.violinjudy.com

ISBN: 978-1-960674-31-9

Violin Judy's
VERY FUN VIOLIN LIBRARY

The Accidental Axolotl is composed for Very Fun Violin LEVEL D learners or any
learner who has mastered playing fingers on D, A and E strings of the violin.
A level chart is included in the back of this book.

DO`S AND DON`TS FOR VIOLIN:

WASH YOUR HANDS BEFORE YOU PLAY OR PRACTICE VIOLIN.

PLACE YOUR MUSIC ON THE STAND BEFORE YOU OPEN YOUR VIOLIN CASE.

HOLD YOUR BOW WITH THE FROG OR STICK. AVOID TOUCHING THE HAIR. NATURAL OILS ON CLEAN HANDS CAN RUB OFF ON YOUR BOW WHICH PREVENTS ROSIN FROM STICKING TO YOUR BOW.

WHEN TUNING YOUR VIOLIN USE THE FINE TUNERS FOR SMALL PITCH CHANGES. REMEMBER RIGHTY-TIGHTY FOR THE PITCH TO GO HIGHER AND LEFTY-LOOSEY FOR THE PITCH TO GO LOWER.

DON`T LET YOUR VIOLIN "WIGGLE" BACK AND FORTH WHEN YOU PLAY. YOUR VIOLIN SHOULD STAY STILL AND FLAT AS A TABLETOP. THE VIOLIN IS THE CONSTANT (STAYING THE SAME) AND THE BOW IS THE VARIABLE (CHANGING.)

ROSIN YOUR BOW A LOT WHEN IT`S BRAND NEW. IN THE FUTURE, JUST THREE SWIPES UP AND DOWN BEFORE YOU PRACTICE EACH DAY IS ENOUGH.

DON`T HOLD YOUR BOW BY THE HAIR! THIS WILL RUIN YOUR BOW HAIR WITH THE NATURAL OILS ON YOUR FINGERS

USE A MUSIC STAND! IT WILL HELP YOU HOLD YOUR VIOLIN FLAT LIKE A TABLE AND YOU`LL SOUND BETTER!

WHOLE NOTE

"WHOLE NOTE HOLD IT"
4 BEATS

HALF NOTE

"HOLD ME"
2 BEATS

QUARTER NOTE

"QUARTER"
1 BEAT

QUARTER REST

"QUARTER"
1 BEAT OF REST

SHARP

RAISES A NOTE 1/2 STEP
TO THE RIGHT

FLAT

LOWERS A NOTE 1/2
TO THE LEFT

AXEL AXOLOTL

TREBLE CLEF

VIOLINS PLAY NOTES
IN THIS CLEF

A VIOLIN

HALF REST

HOLD 2 BEATS

QUARTER REST

HOLD 1 BEAT

REPEAT SIGN

PLAY AGAIN

DOUBLE BAR LINE

THE END OF THE
PIECE

NATURAL

NOTE RETURNS
TO THE
"NORMAL" PLACE

BAR LINE

CREATES MEASURES
DON'T STOP!

DOTTED HALF NOTE

"HOLD ME PLEASE"
THREE BEATS

6

THAT'S GREAT, YOU **KNOW** "3 ON G" IS C, "3 ON D" IS G, "3 ON A" IS D AND "3 ON E" IS A! NOW, HOW ABOUT YOUR **HOMEWORK**?

I PRACTICED JINGLE BELLS!

AXEL! THAT HASN'T BEEN HOMEWORK SINCE **DECEMBER**!

I KNOW, BUT I JUST **LOVE** THAT SONG!
BUT I ALSO TURNED JINGLE BELLS INTO HALLOWEEN MUSIC!
SEE ALL THE ORANGE ARROWS? THAT MEANS TO PLAY LOW 1 ON D.
IT MAKES IT SOUND SPOOKY!

AXEL, THAT IS AMAZING! THIS IS EXACTLY
WHAT I WANTED TO TEACH YOU ABOUT TODAY!

IT IS? YIPPEE! THAT MAKES ME
SO HAPPY I WANT TO BOUNCE!

HEY AXEL, THERE'S A <u>SECRET CODE</u> THAT MUSICIANS USE INSTEAD OF THOSE ORANGE ARROWS, AND IT WILL MAKE YOUR MUSIC EASIER TO READ! THIS SYMBOL IS CALLED A <u>FLAT</u> AND INSTEAD OF WRITING IT BEFORE <u>EVERY</u> NOTE, YOU CAN JUST WRITE IT <u>ONCE</u> AT THE BEGINNING OF EACH MEASURE TO LOWER A NOTE A 1/2 STEP. IT LOOKS LIKE A SMOOSHED LETTER B. TRY IT!

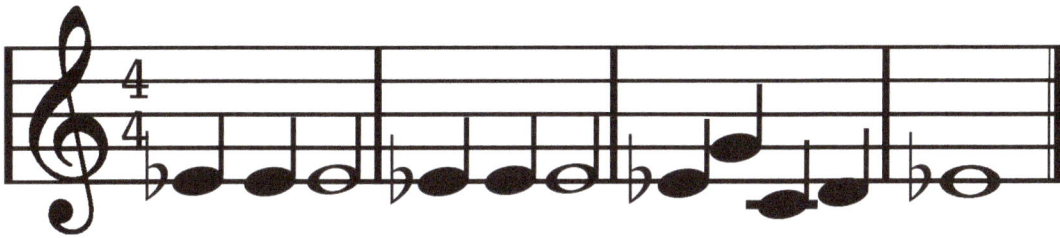

WOW! THAT IS ALOTOL EASIER! AND I DON'T HAVE TO WRITE THEM ON EVERY NOTE !

YOU CAN USE FLATS TO MAKE ALMOST ALL THE MUSIC YOU'VE LEARNED SOUND "SPOOKY". WE CALL SPOOKY, SAD OR MELANCHOLY SOUNDING MUSIC "MINOR." WHEN THE MUSIC SOUNDS HAPPY WE CALL THAT "MAJOR!" NOW ABOUT YOUR LESSON...

HEY, TEACHER, I HAVE ANOTHER QUESTION!

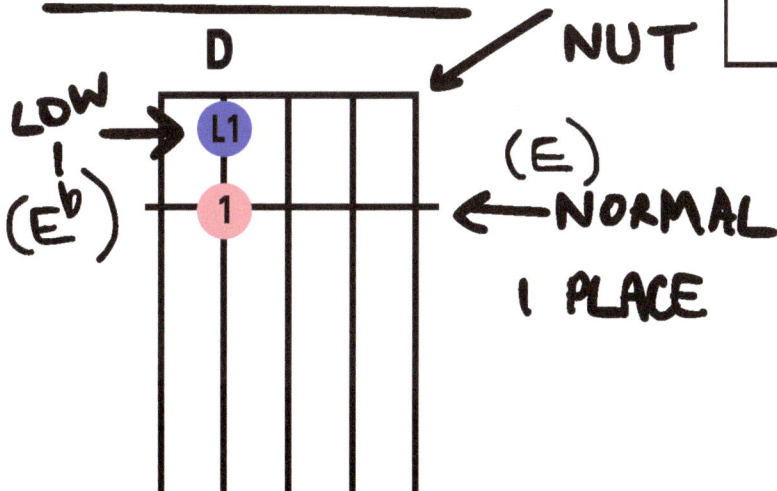

HOW CAN I MAKE A NOTE GO HIGHER? IS THERE A SECRET CODE FOR THAT?

Axel's Notes

D

NUT

LOW

L1

(E♭)

1

(E)

NORMAL

1 PLACE

7

HELP AXEL DRAW FLATS IN FRONT OF THESE SPACE NOTES, THEN WRITE THE NAME OF THE NOTE IN THE BOX!

HELP AXEL DRAW FLATS IN FRONT OF THESE LINE NOTES, THEN WRITE THE NAME OF THE NOTE IN THE BOX!

STOP BOUNCING FOR A BIT AND I'LL SHOW YOU A SHARP SYMBOL

OH SURE, I KNOW THIS! I PLAY SHARP ALL THE TIME WITH MY BEST FRIEND OCTAVIUS!

YOU'RE THINKING OF TIC-TAC-TOE: THAT'S A GAME. SHARPS ARE ANOTHER SECRET CODE OF MUSICIANS!

A SHARP MAKES A NOTE HIGHER BY A 1/2 STEP. WHEN YOU SEE THIS SYMBOL YOU'LL MOVE YOUR FINGER 1/2 STEP HIGHER-CLOSER TO YOUR NOSE!

SHARP

AXEL-AWESOME! I CAN'T WAIT TO TRY IT OUT IN THIS PIRATE SONG I MADE UP YESTERDAY. CAN YOU HELP ME WRITE THOSE SHARP THINGYS IN?

SURE: SHARPS ARE PRETTY EASY TO WRITE: TWO STRAIGHT LEGS AND THE ARMS GO UP AND TO THE RIGHT LIKE A DAB!

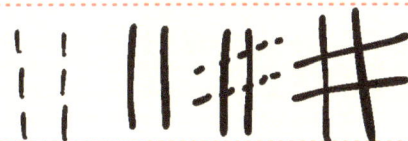

YO HO HO AND A BOTTLE OF CHUM, WITH

YOU MY FRIEND WE WILL LAUGH 'TILL WE'RE DONE!

AXEL'S WORKOUT MUSIC

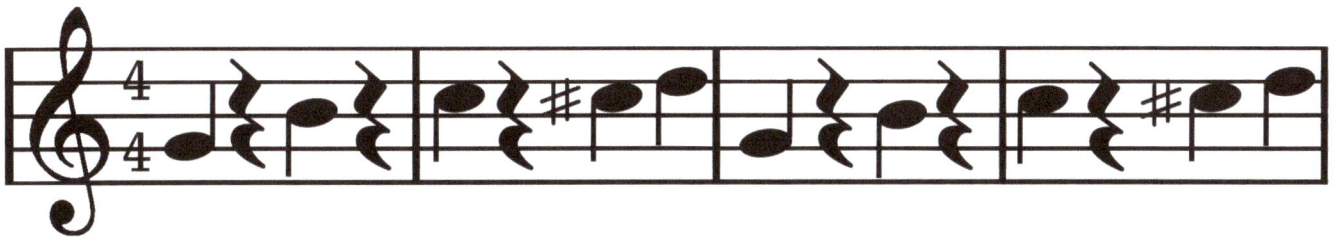

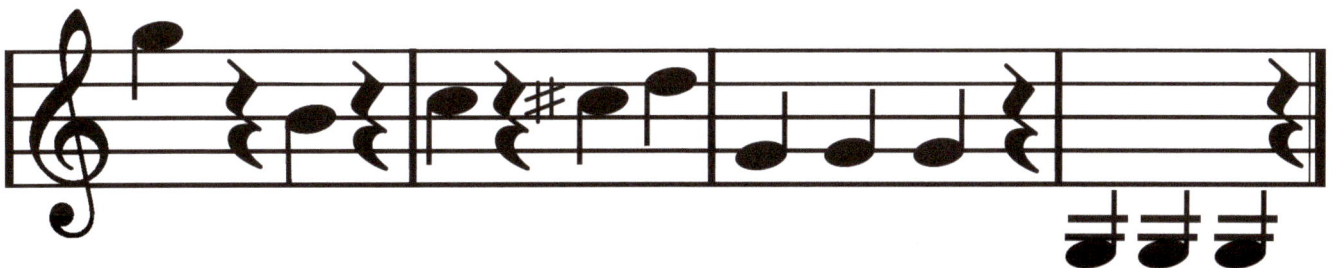

HELP AXEL DRAW SHARPS IN FRONT OF THESE SPACE NOTES, THEN WRITE THE NAME OF THE NOTE IN THE BOX!

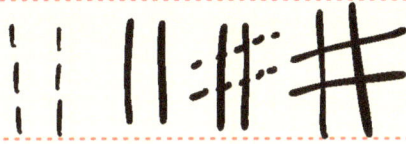

WOW, THAT'S A GREAT WAY TO USE SHARPS! NOW, ABOUT YOUR HOMEWORK FROM LAST WEEK....

SURE, BUT FIRST I HAVE ANOTHER QUESTION...

YES AXEL.....

WHAT IF I DON'T WANT THE NOTE TO BE SHARP OR FLAT ANYMORE? CAN I JUST WRITE "NO" IN FRONT OF THE NOTE?

THAT'S ACTUALLY A GREAT QUESTION! THERE IS ONE MORE SPECIAL SYMBOL I NEED TO TEACH YOU FIRST...

SPECIAL SYMBOL? LIKE AN EMOJI?

NOPE! THE LAST SECRET CODE MUSICIANS USE IS CALLED A NATURAL. IT TURNS A NOTE BACK TO NORMAL! LIKE WHEN YOU TAKE OFF YOUR HALLOWEEN COSTUME!

OH SURE, THAT MAKES SENSE. REMEMBER LAST YEAR WHEN I DRESSED UP LIKE A ZOMBIE? THIS YEAR I WANT TO BE A WITCH!

YES, I REMEMBER YOUR HALLOWEEN COSTUMES, BUT LET'S GET BACK TO MUSIC! TO DRAW A NATURAL SIGN YOU START BY DRAWING A LETTER L

I'M GOOD AT THOSE THERE ARE <u>ALOTL</u> IN MY NAME!

VERY FUNNY! THE NEXT STEP IS TO DRAW AN UPSIDE DOWN L. THIS PART IS TRICKY SO LOOK AT MY EXAMPLE CAREFULLY.

AND THAT'S ALL I HAVE TO DO TO MAKE THE NOTE NORMAL? THAT'S EASY!

SURE, JUST REMEMBER THAT A BAR LINE ERASES ALL THE FLATS AND SHARPS TOO, SO YOU ONLY NEED A NATURAL IF IT'S IN THE SAME MEASURE WITH A FLAT OR SHARP BEFORE IT.

REMEMBER, ONCE A NOTE IS SHARP OR FLAT, IT STAYS THAT WAY UNTIL THE BAR LINE ERASES IT!

WHOA, I'M CONFUSED.

NO WORRIES, CHECK THIS OUT: SEE THE BIG PINK ERASERS ON THE BAR LINES? IMAGINE THOSE ERASERS ARE THERE ALL THE TIME, ERASING YOUR SHARPS AND FLATS!

HELP AXEL FIGURE OUT HOW MANY SHARPS OR FLATS ARE IN EACH MEASURE, THEN WRITE THE NUMBER IN THE BOX

AXEL'S LULLABY

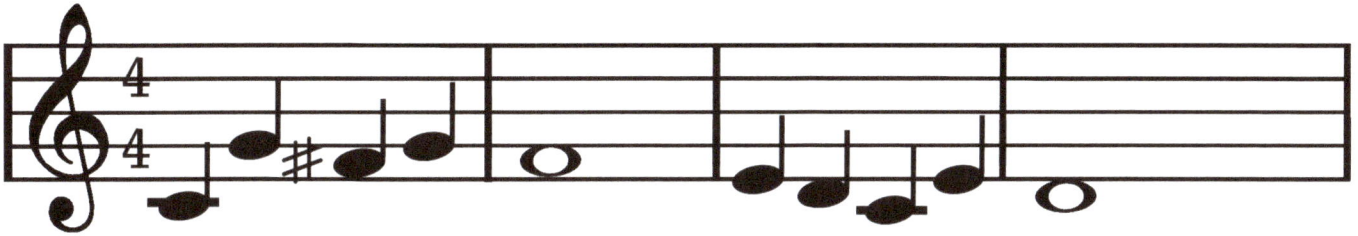

HEY AXEL, DON'T FALL ASLEEP! YOUR
LESSON IS ALMOST OVER THEN YOU
CAN GO HOME AND TAKE A NAP!

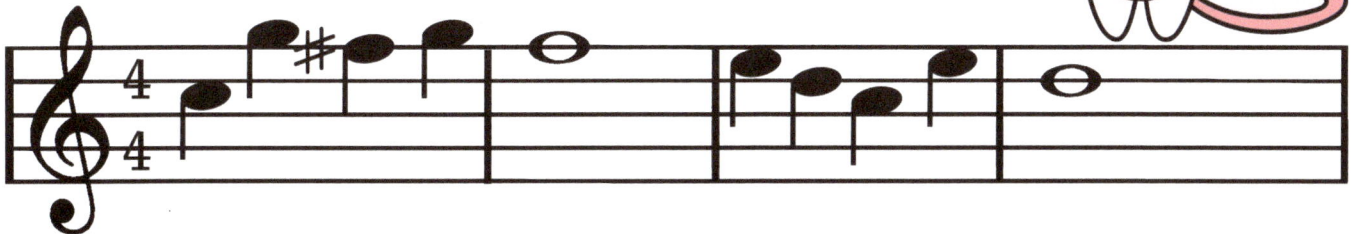

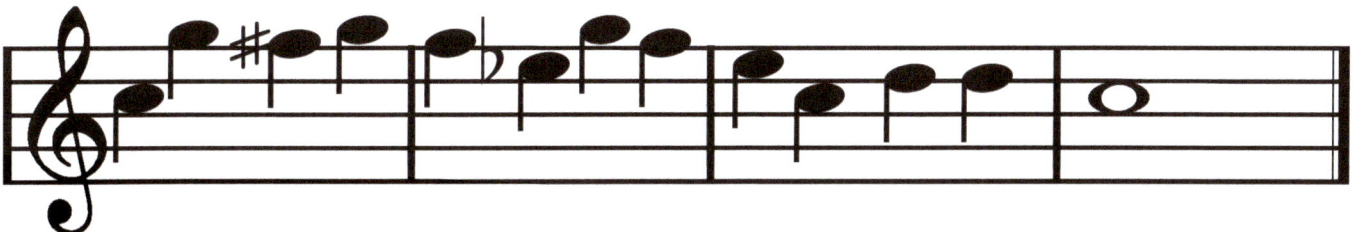

HEY, I THINK I'VE GOT IT!

GREAT, NOW LET'S PLAY THIS PIECE THAT HAS ALOTL, I MEAN, A LOT OF ACCIDENTALS!

DID YOU SAY AXOLOTOLS?

NO, ACCIDENTALS! SAY "AX-I-DENT-TALS." THAT'S WHAT WE CALL SHARPS, FLATS AND NATURALS.

SHARP-RAISES A NOTE 1/2 STEP

NATURAL-RETURN TO THE NORMAL KEY

FLAT-LOWERS A NOTE 1/2 STEP

SHARP LOOKOUT

THIS PIECE USES LOW 2 (G NATURAL) ON THE E STRING.
THIS MEANS PUT 2 AND 1 FINGERS SNUGGLED CLOSE TOGETHER!

Every time I play vi – o –lin I will look for sharp signs!

I know that they make notes higher, and i draw just four lines.

Two lines go-ing down, up, two a-cross and up, yup!

Every time I play vi – o –lin I will look for sharp signs!

Ev-ery time I practice I will know about these signs!

EXTRA SHARP LOOKOUT

HAVE YOU EVER PLAYED A TRANSPOSED PIECE?

THIS PIECE IS LIKE "SHARP LOOKOUT" ON THE PREVIOUS PAGE

BUT HAS A DIFFERENT STARTING PITCH.

Every time I play vi – o –lin   I will look for   sharp signs!

I know that they make notes higher, and i draw just four lines.

Two lines go-ing down, up, two a-cross and up, yup! Every time I

play vi – o –lin   I will look for   sharp signs!   Every time I

practice I will   know about these signs!

26

SHARP ATTACK

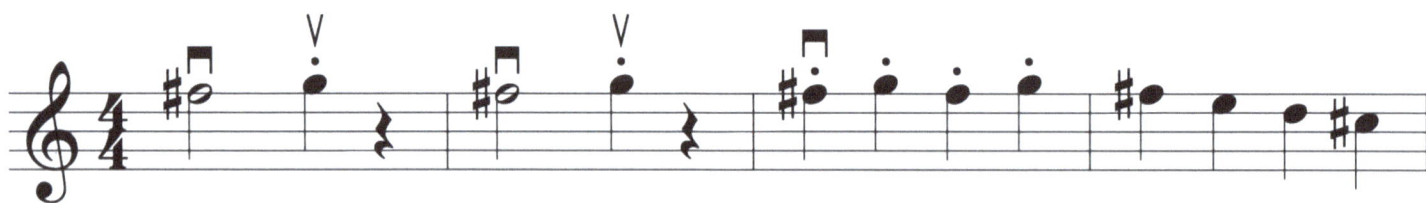

Thanks for teach - ing me ab-out these sharps!

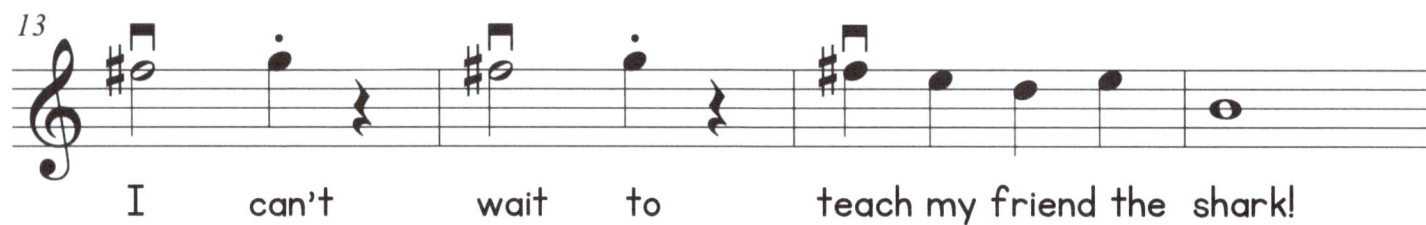

I can't wait to teach my friend the shark!

Just like a sec-ret code, I'm in awe,

NORMALIZE NATURALS

AXEL, I LOVED YOUR CONCERT, YOU SOUNDED AMAZING! YOU'VE LEARNED SO MUCH TODAY! JUST REMEMBER: A SHARP MAKES A NOTE 1/2 STEP HIGHER, A FLAT MAKES A NOTE 1/2 STEP LOWER AND A NATURAL RETURNS THE NOTE TO THE "NORMAL" PLACE. NOW YOU JUST NEED TO PRACTICE YOUR HOMEWORK THIS WEEK! OKAY!? AXEL? AXEL.....

ACCIDENTAL MAZE

Help Axel find his way to his delicious fish dinner through the accidental maze by connecting the notes in order:

BOOK LEVEL CHART FOR THE **VERY FUN VIOLIN LIBRARY**

VIOLIN GRADE	FUN VIOLIN LEVEL	MAIN CONCEPTS
PRE-TWINKLE	A	PRE-TWINKLE RHYTHMS, FINGERS 1,2,3 ON A FINGER 1 ON E
LEVEL 1A	B	NOTE READING 1,2,3 ON A OPEN D & 1 ON E
LEVEL 1B	C	NOTE READING ON D, A & E STRINGS, FINGER 4
LEVEL 2A	D	NOTE READING ON ALL STRINGS
LEVEL 2B	E	INTRO TO 3RD POSITION & VIBRATO

Violin Judy

Mrs. Judy Naillon, or "ViolinJudy" is a dedicated and enthusiastic independent piano and violin teacher, composer, and professional violinist. Her work consists of her large private music studio, as well as playing with her string quartet and Wichita Symphony Orchestra. She served as a church musician for over 20 years and is active in leadership in the musicians' union. She loves coming up with creative ideas to help both students and teachers be successful and blogs about it all at www.ViolinJudy.com and for Alfred's Music Publishers. When she is not writing new books she loves spending time with her family and little dog Pom.

CERTIFICATE

OF ACHIEVEMENT

This awarded to :

----

for the achievement of the completion of:

_____   _____
Teacher   Date